To my love!

Joseph,

Here is a gift so that you can know and learn more of my hometown.

I look forward to our future trips to New York City together and to our awesome success in our new GFM EastCoast office.

I love you

Your Queen
Yvette

Yvette Paez

NEW YORK
THE GROWTH OF THE CITY

CHARTWELL
BOOKS, INC.

This edition published in 2007 by

CHARTWELL BOOKS, INC.
A Division of
BOOK SALES, INC.
114 Northfield Avenue
Edison, New Jersey 08837

ISBN-13: 978-0-7858-2209-7
ISBN-10: 0-7858-2209-7

© 2007 Compendium Publishing, 43 Frith Street, London, Soho, W1V 4SA, United Kingdom

Cataloging-in-Publication data is available from the Library of Congress

Printed and bound in China

Design: Ian Hughes/Compendium Design

Page 2: Staten Island ferry headed for Manhattan, June 1970.
Page 4: Detail of the face of the Statue of Liberty.

Contents page

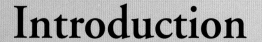

Introduction

The classic skyline of New York City, taken
before the destruction of the elegant and
monumental twin towers of the World
Trade Center by terrorists.

Introduction

New York City as we know it today ranks as one of the world's most populous and influential. With the glittering skyscrapers of Manhattan Island at its heart, the metropolis is made up of five boroughs—Bronx, Brooklyn, Queens, and Staten Island are the other four—which are home to over eight million people, making New York the largest city in the United States by a comfortable margin of about four million. Within its 322 square miles is an incredibly diverse cultural landscape including the Puerto Rican community of Lower East Side, Chinatown, Africa-American dominated Harlem, Little Italy, middle-class Brooklyn, Bohemian Greenwich Village, and many more. Its architecture ranges from Colonial homes such as the Morris-Jumel Mansion used as a headquarters by George Washington, and Victorian tenements that were once densely packed with immigrants, to towers of glass and steel and works of modern architectural genius, such as Frank Lloyd Wright's masterpiece, the Guggenheim Museum. The city's businesses and corporations are central to the American economy as well as that of the rest of the globe, while its designers, writers, artists, filmmakers, and musicians are always looked to for inspiration. Nowhere in the world is quite like New York. With its tarnished glitz and gritty sophistication, the deep ravines of its skyscraper lined streets, and intimate neighborhoods, it is a unique and mythical city.

All this is quite an achievement for a settlement that was founded with the establishment of a simple fur trading post in 1625, but the engine of New York's growth and evolution has been unstoppable. The fledgling town, then Dutch-owned New Amsterdam, found its feet under the rule of the benevolently despotic Peter Stuyvesant, who arrived in 1647, and was soon growing rapidly. Ease of access for fur traders to the American interior via the Hudson River, the early industry of flour milling, and the protection offered by Fort Amsterdam fuelled its expansion. Even in these early days the town fostered a multicultural community, the first Jewish settlers arriving in 1654. The remnants of the Dutch colony can still be felt in the twisting streets of Lower Manhattan, a legacy of the days when buildings were erected wherever seemed convenient, and in the names of Broadway (from the Dutch *Breede Wegh*) as well as Wall Street, named for the wooden fence that once kept the settlement's inhabitants safe from attack.

Dutch rule was overthrown by the British in 1664 and after a few years of being exchanged back and forth, the settlement became permanently British in 1680, now named New York. By this time the

RIGHT: This painting by Joost Hartgers is thought to be one of the first ever views of Manhattan Island and the tiny settlement of New Amsterdam. Dating to between 1626 and 1628 it would have been completed shortly after Peter Minuit had purchased the island from its Native American inhabitants for twenty-four dollars worth of goods. The picture shows some of New Amsterdam's earliest buildings, including 1624's fort, a windmill, and about twenty small houses. Around the island are Dutch trading vessels and Native American canoes.

townsfolk had built the Great Dock on the East River and the town was poised to take advantage of increasing trade with other East Coast colonies as well as further afield in Europe and the West Indies. Although initially overshadowed by Boston and Philadelphia, the town continued to grow. By 1700 there were 7,000 New Yorkers living in increasingly crowded Lower Manhattan and the ninety-two cannons of the Battery intimidated any potential invaders.

In the years up to the revolution the town flourished; ships were being built in the new shipyard; New York's sons could be educated at King's College (now Columbia University); a theater provided entertainment; and the city's earliest publishing enterprise, the *New-York Gazette*, began disseminating news among its readers. In addition, wealthy merchants and farmers were now building ever-larger brick houses, both on Manhattan and out in the fields of what would become Bronx, Queens, and Brooklyn. By 1760 the island's burgeoning population, which was now approaching 20,000, was served by a professional police force.

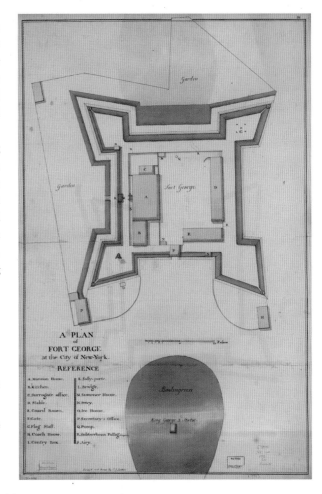

LEFT: The city of New York as it appeared in 1731, with a British Union Jack being proudly flown from the stern of the warship. The view shows the old Fort Amsterdam, which was renamed Fort James by the first British governor, Richard Nicholls, in 1664. By 1714 it was known as Fort George. Behind the fort a much larger town can be seen dotted with the spires of churches.

RIGHT: A plan of Fort George, thought to have been drawn in 1773, with a key to the buildings within its walls. The fort had an eventful history lasting over a century and a half. It was briefly recaptured by the Dutch between 1673 and 1674, caught fire in 1741, captured by revolutionary American forces in 1775, partly destroyed in 1776, and was finally demolished in 1790.

11

LEFT: "New York (and Brooklyn)" by X. Simpson shows Manhattan in 1855. Note at the left edge of Battery Park what was Fort Clinton. Built between 1808 and 1811 on an island know as West Battery, it was redundant after the War of 1812 and later became a restaurant, opera house, and theater. Almost directly above the fort is the recently completed Trinity Church, looking over Broadway down Wall Street.

RIGHT: This aerial photograph of Manhattan taken in the late 1920s shows a city beginning to reach upward, making the best use of available land as real estate prices rose and leading the way in the construction of skyscrapers. In Lower Manhattan, Trinity Church is now obscured by towers around Wall Street and Midtown is also beginning to rise.

OVERLEAF: The same view as page 12 circa three decades later shows how quickly New York was growing during this era. Fort Clinton has now been joined to Manhattan Island by landfill, the Brooklyn Bridge (completed 1883) spans the East River, Central Park (1858) provides green space in the center of Manhattan, and the Metropolitan Museum of Art (1880) can be seen on the park, facing Fifth Avenue.

Despite New York's rapid growth, these were turbulent times for the American colonies straining under the burden of unfair British taxes. New York's citizens first came to blows with British troops in 1770 and soon after the advent of war in 1775 American forces took the city. Despite this early victory, the revolutionary army could not spare the men to hold the city and it was left to the British until the war ended in 1783. Soon after though, it was honored to become the temporary capital of the new nation and hosted the inauguration of George Washington, the United States' first president.

Where New York's expansion had been quick before now it stepped up a gear. Trade increased and the population, buoyed by rising European immigration, tripled in the final years of the eighteenth century. As the new century dawned New York was set to take the world by storm and it didn't disappoint. The Erie Canal opened up a waterway to the Great Lakes and beyond in 1825 and the

LEFT: The Flatiron Building nears completion. Opened in 1902, the distinctive triangular building was New York's first true skyscraper. The odd vortex of winds that it causes soon became famous for blowing women's skirts above their waists and for many years a policeman could usually be found here moving on voyeuristic men.

RIGHT: Aerial view of the tip of Manhattan in 1942.

new steamships pioneered by Robert Fulton on the Hudson in 1807 meant that goods could be quickly transported to the West. Where the city's merchants had previously been wealthy, a legion of tycoons appeared whose goods could be easily dispatched around the world. Men like John Jacob Astor epitomized the lure of New York to many poor and downtrodden around the world. Born in Germany in 1763, he came to the city at the age of twenty and initially worked as a baker's boy. His entrepreneurial skills next led him to the fur business and as profits increased he invested in his own ships as well as buying up Manhattan farmland, which became prime real estate as the city marched up the island. Banks, insurance companies, and other financial institutions also sprang up during this period, laying the foundations for the city's future as a hub of finance. The face of New York also changed dramatically during the nineteenth century. In 1811 it was decided that all new building would take place on a strict grid pattern. A fire in 1835 swept away many of the original buildings and they were replaced with ever more fancy homes demanded by the business elite, while the middle classes took to living in the new brownstone rowhouses. New immigrants and the poor were bundled into overcrowded and unsanitary tenement buildings in the city's less salubrious districts such as Five Points and Hell's Kitchen. New York took center stage for a World's Fair in 1853 and five years later Macy's opened its opulent doors for the first time to New Yorkers who could now also take a break from business in leafy Central Park.

However great the city's success, it was as nothing to what lay ahead. The final decades of the nineteenth century after the Civil War saw money pouring into the city from every corner of the globe and filling the city

coffers. Businessmen, industrialists, and city officials responded by lavishing this extravagant wealth on ambitious building projects and public works. Just a few of the buildings to date from this time include the first Grand Central depot, Bloomingdale's, St. Patrick's Cathedral, Brooklyn Bridge, Madison Square Garden, Carnegie Hall, the Dakota (New York's first luxury apartments and later home to many celebrities, including John Lennon), the Metropolitan Museum of Art, and the Waldorf-Astoria Hotel. A small island in New York Harbour also welcomed another new arrival from Europe; the Statue of Liberty, a gift from the French people, was unveiled by President Grover Cleveland in 1886. As the century drew to a close New York became suddenly bigger than ever. Brooklyn, and the areas that would become known as Bronx, Queens, and Staten Island were incorporated into "Greater New York" in 1898. The city's population rocketed to three million (two thirds of whom lived on Manhattan) in one stroke of the pen.

As New York entered its fourth century the skyline so recognizable today began to take shape. First came the Flatiron Building of 1902. Relatively squat by New York's later standards, this elegant building nevertheless signaled the beginning of the age of the skyscraper. It would be followed by such iconic towers as the Woolworth Building, Chrysler Building, the mighty Empire State Building, and the Rockefeller Center. The city was going down as well as up, too. Work on the subway system began in 1900.

The first half of the twentieth century would present New York with some difficult times—two world wars, the Great Depression, and the Prohibition years. Despite these setbacks it continued to set the pace for the rest of the world. Glitz, glamour, and spectacle could have been New

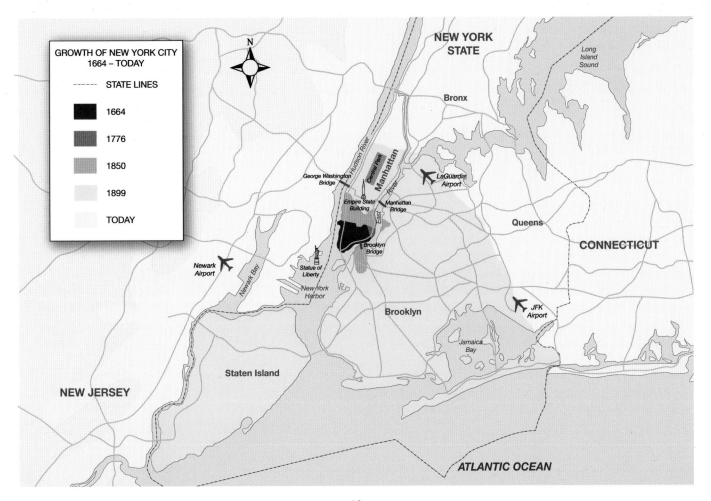

GROWTH OF NEW YORK CITY
1664 – TODAY

- - - STATE LINES

1664
1776
1850
1899
TODAY

N

NEW YORK STATE

Long Island Sound

Bronx

Hudson River

Central Park

Manhattan

LaGuardia Airport

Queens

CONNECTICUT

George Washington Bridge

Empire State Building

Manhattan Bridge

East River

Brooklyn Bridge

Newark Airport

Newark Bay

Statue of Liberty

New York Harbor

JFK Airport

Brooklyn

Jamaica Bay

Staten Island

NEW JERSEY

ATLANTIC OCEAN

York's watchwords. Broadway offered a myriad glittering musical shows, typified by the Ziegfeld Follies, Harlem's Cotton Club presented the great Jazz stars, and all over town people ignored the ban on booze and continued to party in illegal speakeasies.

The second half of the century was not without its problems either, including soaring crime rates and the city's near bankruptcy in the seventies. The city continued to grow though, constructing new landmarks that further enhanced its skyline and cache, including 1959's Guggenheim Museum and, in 1973, the twin titans of the World Trade Center. By the eighties it was party time again with business booming once more and new skyscrapers, such as yuppie king Donald Trump's Trump Tower, appearing everywhere. The city also began looking to its heritage, renovating previously run down areas and revamping Times Square.

Nothing in New York's history could have prepared it for the morning of September 11, 2001 when two airplanes flew out of the blue sky and into the towers of the World Trade Center, destroying them, and with them the lives of thousands. Such devastation is not to be forgotten or easily recovered from, yet in the years since, New York, with typical courage and grit, has not stopped looking to the future, planning new architectural wonders, including the World Trade Center's replacement, the Freedom Tower.

The following pages present a pictorial view of New York's history, from the seventeenth century to the twenty-first. It is a story of dynamic energy and extravagant excess, of a city always evolving, adapting, and growing.

RIGHT: A tiny Dutch settlement less than four hundred years ago, New York City today boasts the most famous skyline in the world. This aerial view includes the curved reflective façade of 17 State Street, at the foot of which is the US Custom House. Behind it is the green pyramid-topped 40 Wall Street. In Battery Park, Fort Clinton still exists and today provides Manhattan's National Park Service with a vistors' center.

Colonial New York: 1600-1775

This painting, called "New Amsterdam, Now New York, on the Island of Manhattan" dates to the mid 1660s and shows a British warship firing cannon upon a smaller Dutch vessel. Never having turned a profit for the Dutch West India Company, New Amsterdam was written off as a bad investment by the Dutch and never adequately defended. When a British invasion fleet arrived on August 26, 1664, Peter Stuyvesant surrendered the colony without a fight.

Colonial New York: 1600-1775

To early explorers the island known to its native Algonquin inhabitants as *Man-a-hat-a*, which translates as "the island of hills," must have seemed an unprepossessing place. Giovanni da Varrazano hardly bothered to glance at the island when he became the first European to navigate New York Harbor in 1524 and Henry Hudson did little more than chart its position in 1609 while sailing up the river in search of a passage to Asia. However, by the second decade of the seventeenth century, Europe was waking up to the natural riches of the New World, particularly the valuable furs of its abundant wildlife that could be traded for a few odds and ends with the locals. When the Dutch West India Company established a trading post on the island in 1625 it was with the explicit intention of gathering as much fur as possible to send back to Europe. The next century and a half would see this relatively small island become one of the most important cities in Colonial America, a bustling little metropolis with a busy port, beautiful churches, and its own college. It grew slowly at first, and even by 1775 almost all of New York's inhabitants were concentrated in Lower Manhattan, but at the onset of the Revolutionary War, the town that had begun with a tiny collection of wooden homes clustered around a fort had a population of 20,000, a theater, its own newspaper, a police force, roomy mansions for its wealthy farmers and merchants, and a bright future.

RIGHT: This 1868 painting commemorates the arrival of Henry Hudson's ship the *Halve Maen* (*Half Moon*) in New York Bay in 1609. Funded by the Dutch East India Company, Hudson became the first to chart the area and established the Dutch claim.

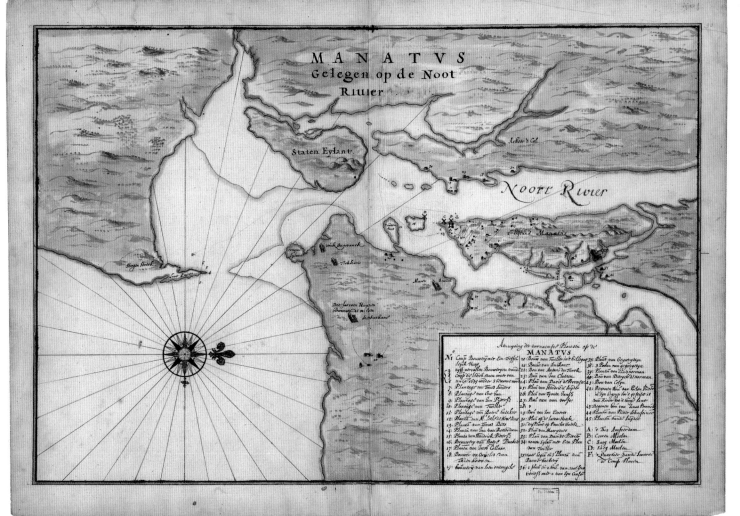

MANATVS
Gelegen op de Noot Riuier

Staten Eylant.

Achter 't Col.

Noort Riuier

't Eÿland Manathans

roeck Duÿuenck

Tekkenis

Hoogen Bodek

t'Lang Eÿlant

Manee

Deze Jacoben Huÿsen
Gommers cÿen M. Pete
dickueslant

LEFT: Constructed in 1652, this earth and timber wall marked the northern boundary of the European settlement and provided a defense against hostile incursions as well as preventing slaves from escaping. While lending its name to the street that grew up along its length, the wall itself was taken down by the British in 1699.

RIGHT: Built in the early 1660s, the residence of Jacob Leisler, a Dutch West India Company soldier who became a wealthy trader, was New Amsterdam's first brick house. It was situated on "The Strand," today's Whitehall Street.

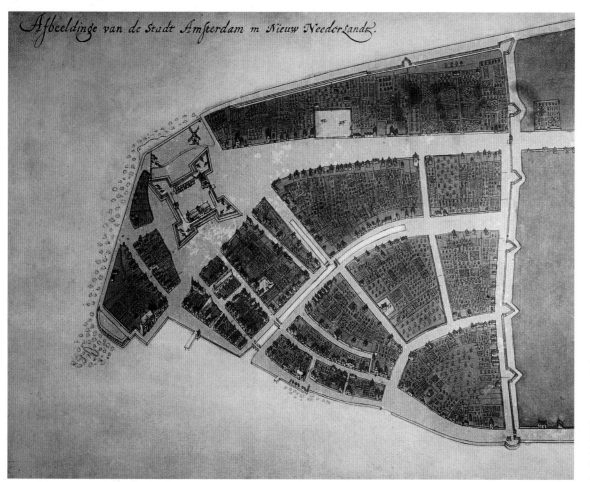

Afbeeldinge van de Stadt Amsterdam in Nieuw Neederlandt.

LEFT: Known as the Castello Plan, this map of New Amsterdam provides a detailed glimpse of the colony in 1660, shortly before being taken over by the British. Individual houses are marked as well as the fort, windmill, parks, and the defensive wall.

RIGHT: Manhattan was not alone in attracting European settlers. The Bowne House, which still stands in Flushing, Queens, is an early farmhouse built by English Quaker John Bowne in 1661. Today it operates as a museum of early settlement.

LEFT: This painting, by J.L.G. Ferris entitled "The Fall of New Amsterdam" shows governor Peter Stuyvesant being begged by residents not to open fire on the British warships that have arrived in the harbor. The governor's instinct was to resist the British, but he yielded to the demands of the townspeople and signed a treaty at his Bouwerie on September 9, 1664. As an interesting side note, Stuyvesant later died on his lands and it is said that the ghostly tap tap of his wooden leg can still be heard at the church of St. Mark's in the Bowery.

CITY HALL AND GREAT DOCK.

RIGHT: The British quickly moved to improve New York's fortunes, which had languished under the Dutch. In 1676 the Great Dock was built, seen here overlooked by City Hall, in order to encourage trade.

A Plan of the City of New York from an actua[l]

North River

To the Honourable
James De Lancey, Esq.
Lieutenant Governor and
Commander In Chief In and over
The Province of NEW YORK
And Territory Depending thereon
In America
This Plan of the City of New
YORK Is Humbly Dedic. By
Your Honours Most Obed.
Humble Servent
G. Duyckinck

A Scale of
One

King's Farm

PALISADES

the Out in Lots

Part of it Lay

Common

Kip Street   High Road

WEST WARD

BROAD WAY

NORTH WARD

William Street

MONT GO ME RIE

W A R D

King George

DOCK WARD

SOUTH WARD

Beaver Street

Broad Street

EAST WARD

Nassau Street

Smith Street

William Street

Queen Street

WATER STREET

Tan Yard

WHITE HALL Str.

W. Dock

Dock Street

Hanover Square

Hunters Key

Burnets Key

Rotten Row

Harbour

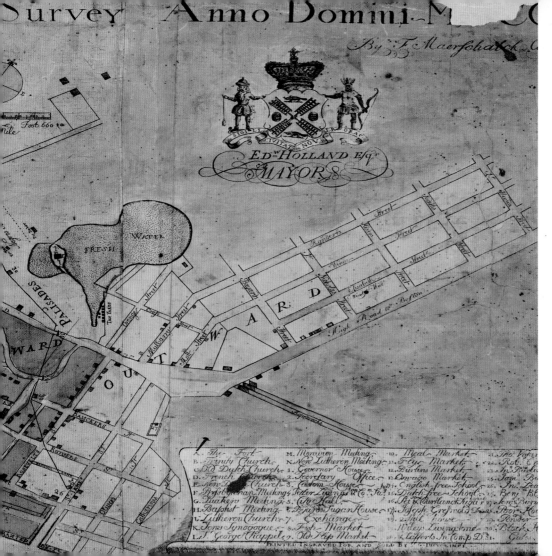

Survey Anno Domini M...

By T. Maerschalck...

Ed.ᵂ Holland Esqʳ
MAYOR.

WATER

FRESH

OUT WARD

PALISADES

MONTGOMERY WARD

WARD

High Road to Boston

A. The Fort.
B. Trinity Church.
C. Old Dutch Church.
D. French Church.
E. New ... Church.
F. Presbyterian Meetings.
G. Quakers Meeting.
H. Baptist Meeting.
I. Lutheren Church.
K. Jews Synagogue.
L. S.ᵗ George Chappel.
M. Moravian Meeting.
N. New Lutheren Meeting.
1. Governor House.
2. Secretary Office.
3. Custom House.
4. Peter Livings & Co Su...
5. City Hall.
6. Bayards Sugar House.
7. Exchange.
8. Fish Market.
9. Old Slip Market.
10. Meal Market.
11. Fly Market.
12. Burlins Market.
13. Oswego Market.
14. English free School.
15. Dutch free School.
16. P.ᵗ & Cumberlandt...
17. Joseph Gresvold...
18. Phil House.
19. Wiley Livingstone.
20. Lafferts In Camp D...

PRINTED ENGRAVED FOR AND SOLD B...

ABOVE: The perfectly maintained Van Cortlandt Mansion dates to 1748 and was once the home of the Frederick Van Cortlandt, the son of a wealthy mercantile family. Constructed with rough stone in the Georgian manner, the house is the oldest in the Bronx and now operates as a museum.

ABOVE: The Morris-Jumel Mansion is a noted Colonial dwelling and the oldest still standing on Manhattan. It was built in 1765 for British Colonel Roger Morris and the estate originally comprised 130 acres. Used as a headquarters by George Washington during the defense of Manhattan in 1776, it was later owned by wine trader Stephen Jumel and his scandalous wife Eliza. The wood-sided mansion is elegantly Classical, with a Palladian portico and now operates as a museum featuring many of the Jumels' possessions, including a bed that Eliza boasted once belonged to Napoleon Bonaparte.

RIGHT: A view of St. Paul's across Broadway today. A beautiful example of Colonial Classical style architecture, complete with original handcarvings, the chapel is now on one of the city's busiest thoroughfares.

A New American City: 1776-1849

Greenwich Village, which had been a sleepy pastoral suburb for many years was transformed by the mid-nineteenth century into a popular residential area. Many new inhabitants came to escape the city's frequent outbreaks of disease and decided to stay.

A New American City: 1776-1849

In 1766 George Washington's Continental Army left New York to British forces despite Washington's victory at the Battle of Harlem Heights on September 16. For the remainder of the conflict it remained in British hands. Scarred by the shelling and numerous fires, one of which burned Trinity Church to the ground, the city emerged from the war battered and bruised, but gave Washington a hero's welcome when he returned in 1783. With the dynamism and tenacity that New Yorkers are renowned for, the new citizens of the United States set about making their city bigger and more successful than ever. New York became the capital of the new country for a while (from 1785 to 1790), banks were chartered, hospitals built, and the Stock Exchange was founded in the Tontine Coffee House. The always busy docks became a forest of masts as ships from around the world unloaded

BELOW: The Tontine Coffee House at Wall and Water streets, was the first home of the New York Stock exchange in 1792. At the end of Wall Street the dock is bristling with ships' masts, indicating the city's growing importance as a center of commerce.

RIGHT: "Washington's Triumphal Entry into New York, Nov. 25th, 1783," by C. Inger records the great general's arrival. Two years later it would be named capital and in 1789 George Washington would be inaugurated at Federal Hall.

their cargoes and took on board American goods. When the Erie Canal opened up the West to trade in 1825, New York swiftly overtook Philadelphia and Boston as the center of trade in the United States. It had already bested its two rivals in terms of size of population in 1823. In order to house all the people who flocked to enjoy the city's success, New York began an inexorable spread up Manhattan, now on a strict grid plan. Previously sleepy pastoral hamlets, such as Greenwich Village were now growing in size, with people who had come to escape New York's regular epidemics electing to stay. In 1835, a devastating fire destroyed many of Lower Manhattan's original buildings, but undeterred New York picked itself up once more. By 1942, the city was served by its first fresh water reservoir and its middle classes were increasingly living in brownstone rowhouses. By the middle of the nineteenth century New York would have been almost unrecognizable to the people who hailed George Washington's triumphal entrance. Nevertheless, such phenomenal prosperity and growth would be eclipsed over the next five decades.

ABOVE: The official residence of the mayor of New York, known as the Gracie Mansion, is sited in Carl Schurz Park at the confluence of the East and Harlem rivers and dates to 1799. The Federal-style mansion was built by Scottish shipping magnate Archibald Gracie and had a chequered history, at one time housing an ice-cream parlor, until it became the mayor's residence in 1942.

RIGHT: This building on Bowling Green was originally planned to house the president before Philadelphia became the US capital. It was completed in 1790 and served as the US Custom House between 1799 and 1815.

Castle Clinton dates to 1811 and was originally a gun emplacement on an island off the lower tip of Manhattan. It quickly became redundant and was later used as a theater. It was here that Jenny Lind famously took to the stage in 1850. In subsequent years landfill has connected the castle to the mainland and it is now a national monument.

Completed in 1812, New York's City Hall is emblematic of the city's growing confidence. Designed by one of the nation's first home-grown architects, John McComb, it reflects the United States' countrywide predilection for Palladian influenced Federal-style architecture.

LEFT: Painted in 1819 by Baron Axel Klinckowstrom, this scene shows a very genteel Broadway looking north east at the junction with Vesey Street. The dazzling white new City Hall building is to the right while just visible at the left of the building are the columns of St. Paul's portico. The empty space at the right of the picture would later be home to Phineas T. Barnum's American Museum (RIGHT) from 1841 to 1865 with its weird and wonderful exhibits, including mermaids and the renowned Tom Thumb. Later the New York city General Post Office (OVERLEAF) was built here. The Woolworth Building would eventually rise at the Barclay Street junction one block up from Vesey Street.

LEFT: The original General Post Office, a fine granite building, was located at the intersection of Broadway and Park Row.

RIGHT: Excavating the foundations of the original New York City Post Office Building.

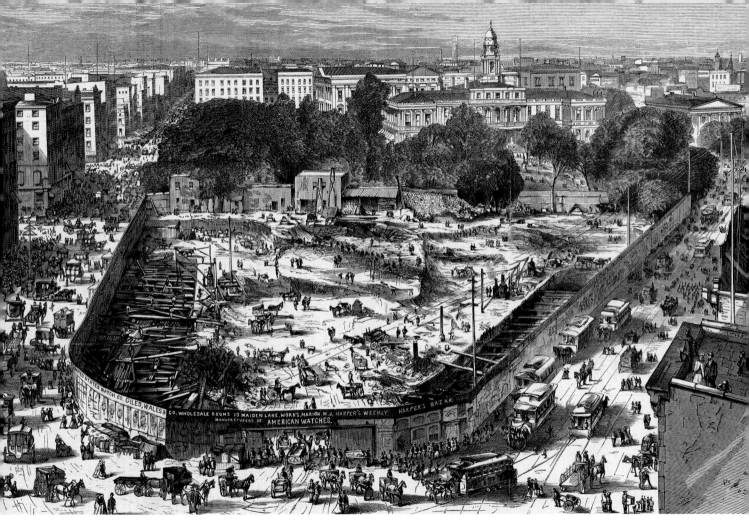

UNITED STATES WATCH CO. GILES, WALES & CO. WHOLESALE ROOMS 13 MAIDEN LANE, WORKS, MARION, N.J. HARPER'S WEEKLY. HARPER'S BAZAR. MANUFACTURERS OF AMERICAN WATCHES.

In 1823 New York City became the most populous metropolis in the United States and
W.G. Wall painted this stunning landscape of New York from Weehawken, the site of an
1804 duel between Vice President Aaron Burr and Alexander Hamilton during which
Hamilton was killed. The city now sprawls further up Manhattan and a taste of its future
can bee seen in the early steamship heading up the Hudson River.

LEFT AND RIGHT: Named for the bowling that was once played here, Bowling Green was New York's first park. It is interesting to compare the illustration of 1830 with a similar view of the park today. The once quiet residential area is now dominated by the shimmering blue column of 17 State Street.

LEFT: Not all of New York was quiet and genteel. This painting from the early 1840s shows the Five Points area in the Lower East Side. The first wave of poverty stricken Irish immigrants, fleeing the potato famine began arriving at this time and made their homes in these slums. Though these people and their descendants would help to build the city as we know it today, life here was initially hard for the immigrants.

RIGHT: This contemporary illustration of Trinity Church dates to 1846, the year when the church was first consecrated. It was the third to be built on the site and owes its wonderful Gothic-Revival design to architect Richard Upjohn. While skyscrapers now dwarf the beautiful building it still stands on Broadway, looking down Wall Street.

At the heart of New York's commercial activity, and its growing wealth, in the mid-nineteenth century was the South Street Seaport. Having been neglected for many years the area has been renovated over the past decades and offers a glimpse into the city's maritime history.

FOR HARTFORD
STEAMERS
CITY OF HARTFORD
AND GRANITE STATE.

113
BLOCK
MAKER

Left: The New York brownstone rowhouses had become popular among the middle classes by the mid-nineteenth century. Built of local sandstone the steps up to the front door meant that a lower level could be used by servants. These classic examples are just off Washington Square.

Below: This view of New York from the spire of St. Paul's was painted in 1849 by Henry Papprill and shows a burgeoning city, though none of the buildings except for church spires exceed four or five stories. Lower Manhattan was now increasingly commercial as many middle class families moved away from the area following a devastating fire in 1845. Across Broadway from the chapel is Barnum's American Museum and shops, banks, brokers, and other businesses line the streets. To the right of center, along Dey Street, is Brady's Daguerrian Miniature Gallery, where the photographer who would become famous for his Civil War images took early daguerreotype portraits of New Yorkers.

The Greatest City in America: 1850-1899

The Greatest City in America: 1850-1899

Often called the Gilded Age, the second half of the nineteenth century saw unprecedented growth in New York. The city was by this time the undisputed center of American commerce and its business leaders lavished their fabulous wealth on opulent headquarters as well as public buildings. Indeed, some of the city's best-loved architectural treasures were erected during this era. The Metropolitan Museum, Carnegie Hall, and the New York Public Library all opened their doors to the public, while tourists and business visitors could stay at the ornate Waldorf-Astoria or Plaza hotels. Of course New York's tycoons also needed suitable stores in which to spend—Macy's and Bloomingdales were founded during this period. The less wealthy could now get around the city by elevated rail above the city streets and by 1858 any of the city's inhabitants could relax with a stroll in Central Park.

Despite all this wealth and luxury, like any city New York had its share of poor, particularly as immigration began to increase, with refugees fleeing the poverty and oppression of old Europe in search of a better life as promised by the newly unveiled Statue of Liberty. The new arrivals were squeezed into tenement buildings in the city's slum areas, such as Five Points in the Lower East Side. Nevertheless, by the time the century drew to an end New York had not only filled Manhattan from end to end but with the addition of the Bronx, Queens, Staten Island, and Brooklyn had become the

world's second largest city. Staggeringly expensive homes filled Fifth Avenue, while New Yorkers could also opt to live in luxury apartments such as offered at the Dakota. Although not without difficulties in the shape of the Civil War, corruption in City Hall, and Stock Exchange panic, these five decades saw New York become the most successful and grandest city in all America.

BELOW: As you might expect from a city with so many wealthy and notable inhabitants, New York boasts one of the world's finest cemeteries, the 400 acres of Woodlawn Cemetery in the Bronx. Established in 1863 Woodlawn's famous graves include those of Irving Berlin, F.W. Woolworth, and Duke Ellington.

PREVIOUS PAGE: This modern photograph of 1883's Brooklyn Bridge serves as a reminder of what an integral part of the New York cityscape the structure, with its striking Gothic arches, has.

RIGHT: A view of Wall Street on October 13, 1857, during a financial panic that saw a suspension of all banking for two months. Trinity Church is still the tallest building on the street. The building with the Palladian portico on the right of the street is Federal Hall, built in 1789.

Central Park

Created out of wasteland, swamps, quarries, and pig farms by the great Frederick Law Olmstead and Calvert Vaux in 1858, the 843 acre Central Park is one of New York's great icons. Its lakes, meadows, and wooded areas bounded by museums and some of the most expensive real estate in the world have starred in many movies and supply a peaceful escape for New Yorkers as well as a venue for sports and entertainment.

RIGHT: An aerial photograph of Central Park looking down Manhattan toward the theater district. The large open field to the left of center is the Sheep Meadow and the building encroaching into the park near the Reservoir is the Metropolitan Museum of Art. Wollman Rink can just be seen on the near right hand side.

LEFT: Bow Bridge is of cast iron and is the work of Vaux. It is one of seven in the park. As well as boating, the lake was used in the nineteenth century for winter skating.

Providing wonderful views across the park and
city from the roof, Belvedere Castle derives its
name from the architectural term "belvedere,"
which is a lookout or observatory. The castle
was designed by Law and Olmstead and follows
the European fashion for follies within carefully
laid out gardens.

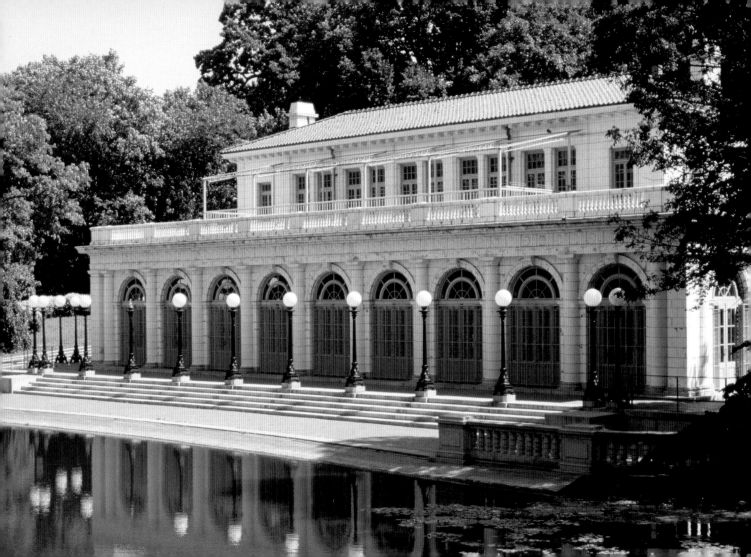

Designed by the same team of Olmstead and Vaux who laid out Central Park, Brooklyn's Prospect Park was completed in 1867 and is considered by some as the finer of the two. Pictured are The Boathouse (now a visitors' center) and the cast iron Olmstead Bridge.

LEFT: 1868 saw the opening of New York's first elevated rail track, on Greenwich Street. This colored photograph, which dates to the turn of the century shows the tracks over the Bowery.

RIGHT New York's American Museum of Natural History overlooks Central Park on the Upper West Side. Like the Met across the park it has outgrown its original building of 1877 and now occupies four complete blocks. The photograph shows the main entrance hall with its skeletons of a Barosaurus being attacked by an Allosaurus.

BELOW AND RIGHT: The exterior of the Metropolitan Museum of Art from an early twentieth century photograph and the Great Hall today. The museum was founded in 1870 by leading New York businessmen and artists and relocated to this site in 1880. The original building has since been almost completely obscured by later additions as the museum's collection has grown to rival any in the world.

RIGHT: The Dakota apartments were the first luxury apartments to be built and set a new trend in housing. Completed in 1884 they were so named because the building was as remote from the city at the time as Dakota. Indeed, until the rest of New York caught up with the building, farm animals were a common sight outside.

Brooklyn Bridge

Work commenced on Brooklyn Bridge on January 3, 1870 and finished in early 1883. The brainchild of John A. Roebling, it was the first to span the East River and connect New York City to Brooklyn and played a vital role in the latter's development. At the time of its completion it was the world's greatest suspension bridge.

RIGHT: An early photograph of construction on the bridge—the near completion of the towers dates it to 1877. Each tower is 276 feet high and built of granite in a Gothic style featuring the two distinctive arches that give the bridge its character. The towers serve to take the weight of the cables and the bridge itself and allowed engineers to build the crossing high enough so that river traffic could pass underneath.

LEFT: Brooklyn Bridge spans 6,016 feet, including the approaches and is 135 feet above the East River at its highest point. When complete it quickly became both a New York icon and a symbol of the city's ambition and know-how. The painting shows the bridge being crossed by horse-drawn carriages, while sailing and steam ships pass easily beneath as planned.

Statue of Liberty

Standing on a small island just off the southern tip of Manhattan, the Statue of Liberty was a gift from the French people to America, conceived by sculptor Frederic-Auguste Bartholdi. On her base is inscribed a poem, "The New Colossus" by Emma Lazarus, the words of which are as powerful today as they were when the statue was unveiled in 1886:

"Give me your tired, your poor,
Your huddled masses yearning to breathe free,
The wretched refuse of your teeming shore.
Send these, the homeless, tempest-tost to me,
I lift my lamp beside the golden door!"

RIGHT: Before being shipped across the Atlantic, Liberty's head was on display in a public park in Paris. With her face modeled on that of Bartholdi's mother, the seven beams radiating from the crown are symbolic of the seven seas and continents.

ABOVE: A rare photograph of construction in Bartholdi's Parisian workshop. This photograph shows a quarter size model of Liberty's left arm. The finished statue was made up of 300 sheets of copper, which give Liberty her distinctive green appearance.

ABOVE: Liberty's first sight of New York harbor, October 28, 1886, the day she was unveiled by President Grover Cleveland.

"Liberty Enlightening the World" is today perhaps the most famous symbol of freedom in the world and certainly the greatest of all New York landmarks.

LEFT: The city's best example of Gothic Revival architecture is the world famous Saint Patrick's Cathedral on Fifth Avenue. The United States' pre-eminent Catholic church was finished in 1888 and features noted works of art glass, such as the Rose Window at the center of the facade, as well as superb examples of sculpture and the Great Bronze Doors, which weigh 20,000 pounds.

RIGHT: The New York Botanical Garden was founded in 1891. Now occupying 250 acres of the Bronx it is one of the world's finest collections of flora. This photograph taken across the Luce Herb Garden shows part of the beautiful Victorian Enid A. Haupt Conservatory.

LEFT: The finest concert hall in the city, and its first, was funded by tycoon philanthropist Andrew Carnegie and opened its doors for the first time in 1891. Now in its second century, the venue continues to attract the world's best orchestras and artists.

RIGHT: Built to commemorate the centenary of George Washington's inauguration, Washington Arch stands on the north side of Washington Square. Designed by Stanford White it was completed in 1895.

LEFT: In 1895 the Olympia, built by Oscar Hammerstein I, became the first theater to open on Broadway, between 44th and 45th streets, setting the standard for the future.

RIGHT: Hand-tinted view of the bustling life on a New York Lower East side street—Mulberry Street—around 1900. At this time it was the thriving center of Italian immigrants.

Immigration

Throughout New York's history the city has drawn immigrants, attracted to its apparent wealth and the promise of freedom, but in the closing decade of the nineteenth century and the first of the twentieth immigration reached an unprecedented peak. In fact about twelve million people passed through the immigration facility on Ellis Island between 1892 and its closure in 1954.

BELOW LEFT AND RIGHT: Most of those who came through Ellis Island—Jews, Italians, Irish, Germans, Scandinavians, and more—initially lived lives of great hardship in New York's poorest areas, such as Lower East Side and Hell's Kitchen. However, these people often provided the muscle and the determination to succeed that took New York on to some of its greatest years. The photograph on the right shows tailors at work in an Elizabeth Street tenement around 1890.

RIGHT: For millions the facility on Ellis Island was the first taste of life in America. Immigrants were processed as quickly as possible, their papers checked and given a cursory medical examination for any obvious signs of sickness. The Ellis Island doctors were proud of the skill with which they could conduct a "six second medical."

LEFT: It is thought that the ancestors of about fifty percent of the United States' population came through Ellis Island. The main building of the complex now serves as a museum, with exhibits that illustrate their experiences.

RIGHT: Under the shadow of the Statue of Liberty this immigrant family looks toward the shore of their new home.

OVERLEAF: The Tenement Museum in Lower East Side features a completely renovated tenement building, complete with furnishings and fittings that help provide a very real experience of how many people squashed together in these buildings would have lived.

New York Grows Up: 1900-1939

New York Grows Up: 1900-1939

By the beginning of the new century, Manhattan's real estate prices were spiraling and in order to make best use of the land developers began to look upward. Beginning in 1902 with the Flatiron Building (properly called the Fuller Building), New York pioneered a new breed of building—the skyscraper. The first of these, such as Cass Gilbert's Woolworth and New York Life Insurance Company buildings were fanciful Gothic and Beaux Arts inspired towers, but as style moved on, the skyscraper found its perfect expression in the bold symmetry of Art Deco, which bequeathed the New York skyline three of the most famous structures in the world—the Chrysler Building, the Empire State Building, and the Rockefeller Center.

This was a dynamic time for the city. While it had always been something of a melting pot, the millions of European immigrants pouring through Ellis Island were becoming assimilated into the city and were joined by increasing numbers of African-Americans from the West and South, adding strong flavors to New York's cultural mix. While large downtown theaters such as Broadway's new Lyceum staged musical spectaculars, Harlem's smaller theaters and clubs introduced the metropolis to Jazz. Drawing white and black audiences from across the city the new music would become the soundtrack for the Prohibition era, during which more affluent New Yorkers, including Mayor Jimmy Walker, decided that a little thing like the law would not stop the good times.

This was also the age of the Great Depression however. After the Wall Street Crash of 1929, poverty grew so bad that many New Yorkers were forced to live in improvised shacks in Central Park. The ever robust city nevertheless had began its recovery under the leadership of Mayor Fiorello La Guardia by the mid-thirties and by the end of the decade New York was back on its feet, hosting its second World's Fair and attracting tens of millions of visitors.

PREVIOUS PAGE: This period saw the construction of some of New York's most famous and beautiful buildings, including the glorious Art Deco towers of the Chrysler and Empire State buildings.

RIGHT: In 1902, New York got its first glimpse of its architectural future with the completion of the Flatiron Building, the city's first skyscraper and at the time the tallest building in the world. Designed by Chicago's famous team of Daniel Burnham and David Root, the Beaux Arts tower is located on a triangular piece of land created by Twenty-third Street, Fifth Avenue, and Broadway.

Pennsylvania Station

On December 12, 1901, Alexander Cassatt, the president of the Pennsylvania Railroad announced his company's plan to construct a tunnel beneath the Hudson, bringing trains into the heart of Manhattan. The tracks would terminate in a grand station at Thirty-fourth Street. The result was Charles McKim's of McKim, Mead, and White's Beaux Arts masterpiece Pennsylvania Station. The station's demolition in the mid sixties to make way for the architecturally lacklustre Madison Square Gardens was a sad loss to the city.

LEFT: In total, six single track tunnels were bored beneath the Hudson and East rivers, connecting the site of the terminal to the Long Island Rail Road via Queens as well as to New Jersey.

RIGHT: As the structure begins to rise its magnificent proportions are evident. The station would feature an awe-inspiring main entrance and a vast and airy main concourse. The main waiting room was modeled after the Roman Baths of Caracalla.

LEFT: Pennsylvania Station nears
completion in 1909. The columned,
Classical-inspired building combined
a sense of monumental magnificence
with a human scale.

RIGHT: The vaulted main concourse
continued the colonnaded feel of the
station, but in elegant steel and glass,
which flooded it with light.

EXIT

The finished station was a pink granite
and travertine jewel of beautifully
proportioned and colonnaded Beaux Arts
architecture, perfectly designed to suit its
purpose.

Unfortunately, by the 1960s the station was no longer profitable and it was torn down in 1966. Penn Station was redesigned beneath the ground while Madison Square Gardens replaced the original overground structure. The subsequent uproar resulted in New York establishing conservation policies to ensure that such an act of vandalism would never happen again.

LEFT: The great wealth generated in New York meant that the city developed some of the world's best shopping. Bloomingdale's first opened its doors in 1872, while Macy's was founded in 1857 on West Fourteenth Street. The department store proved so popular that by 1902 it needed a larger site and it moved to its present address on West Thirty-fourth Street.

RIGHT: New York was not only starting to reach for the skies, but going underground too. This photograph shows city officials, including Mayor George B. McClellan, riding the first subway at City Hall station on October 27, 1904.

LEFT: Once an untouched coastal wilderness, by 1904 Brooklyn's Coney Island was home to no less than three fairgrounds. The combination of thrills and spills and the beach proved a hit with New Yorkers, particularly during the Depression by which time money for vacations was short and Coney Island just a subway ride away.

RIGHT: One of the city's best-loved buildings, the acclaimed New York Public Library opened in 1911. With its fine Beaux Arts-style architecture designed by Carrere & Hastings, the incredible space of the Main Reading Room, nearly ninety miles of shelves, millions of books, and rare manuscripts including Jefferson's copy of the Declaration of Independence, it is one of the world's greatest public libraries as well as one of the best designed.

Much of New York's success is due to its transportation links with the rest of the country, and toward the end of the nineteenth century this meant rail as well as traditional shipping. So busy was railroad tycoon Cornelius Vanderbilt's 1871 station on Forty-second Street that a new terminal was needed to replace it by the beginning of the new century. The result was the beautiful Beaux Arts Grand Central Terminal, which opened in 1913.

LEFT: Stealing the title of tallest building from the Flatiron on its completion in 1913, Cass Gilbert's Woolworth building at 233 Broadway is 792 feet of exquisite Gothic-inspired architecture. The magnificent skyscraper served as the Woolworth company headquarters until 1997. Inside, it is equally as detailed and beautiful, featuring sculpture, marble walls and floors, and a superb ceiling mosaic.

RIGHT: By the mid-1920s many companies had realized the financial possibilities that the motor car represented for New York City. Early taxi companies were owned by the car manufacturers; for many years the most popular and distinctive were made by the Checkered Cab Manufacturing Company.

Harlem in the Jazz Age

By the early twentieth century residential Manhattan reached Harlem, which became a middle-class, white area. However by the end of the first decade housing supply far exceeded the demand of white owners and many of the buildings were leased to African-American New Yorkers or new arrivals from the South and Midwest, who bought with them Jazz and blues. The result was some of the best nightlife nightlife in New York, with venues including the Cotton Club and the Apollo Theater attracting legendary talent and packing in audiences from all over town.

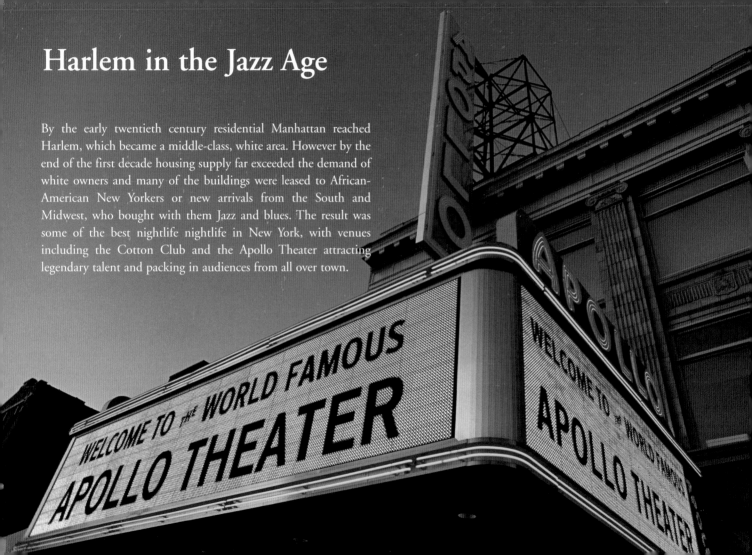

New York Sports

New York has always been a baseball city. Until the 1960s, major league baseball was played at the Polo Grounds—a name that stuck through four different versions of the stadium, the first of which was located at 110th Street and Sixth Avenue. The second was at the northwest corner of the 155th and Eighth intersection; the final two were next door below Coogan's Bluff, and were used by the Giants before their move to San Francisco in 1957.

The images show (LEFT) a poster with the New York Ball Club's home games for the 1887 season. (RIGHT) 24,620 spectators crowd the Polo Grounds to watch Pittsburg vs. New York on May 20, 1905. Finally, (BELOW) a panorama dated October 13, 1910. The

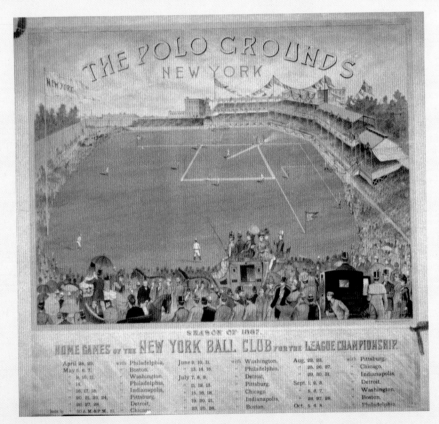

LEFT: Flushing Meadows Park, is located in northern Queens and is the site of the annual US Open tennis competition. In 1997 its new main stadium was opened, named after the famous African-American tennis player, Arthur Ashe, who won the inaugural US Open in 1968.

BELOW: New York has two football teams—the Giants and the Jets—who share a stadium located in East Rutherford, New Jersey. The Jets call the stadium "The Meadowlands" while the Giants—and everyone else—call it "Giants Stadium." Here the New York Jets take on the Indianapolis Colts in 1998.

Built just across the Harlem
River from the Polo Grounds,
which the Yankees' originally
shared with the Giants, Yankee
Stadium opened on April 18,
1923. The first game played
here was against the Boston
Red Sox during which
legendary Babe Ruth hit a
three-run homer and led the
Yankees to a 4-1 victory. Since
then it has been a favorite
venue for baseball fans as well
as hosting other events, such
as a mass given by Pope Paul
VI in 1965.

FAR LEFT: The New York Life Insurance Company Building was designed by Cass Gilbert, who had recently finished the Woolworth Building. Topped by a golden summit, the skyscraper opened for business in 1928.

LEFT: The 1930 Chrysler Building ranks with the Empire State and Statue of Liberty as one of New York's most famous buildings and is undoubtedly the finest work of architect William Van Alen.

RIGHT: Conceived by Walter P. Chrysler, the building was designed to symbolize the cars of which he was so proud. This gargoyle closely resembles the hood ornament of a 1929 model Chrysler Plymouth.

Linking Manhattan to New Jersey, the
George Washington Bridge opened in
1931. The towers at each end were
originally intended to be encased with
stonework, but unfortunately money ran
out, though many believe that the
unadorned steel is more simple and
graceful.

The Empire State Building

Probably the most recognized building anywhere in the world, and a symbol of New York City, the Empire State Building was constructed between 1930 and 1931, by builders who became so nonchalant about the dizzying heights that they worked almost as if at ground level. Topping the Chrysler Building by 408 feet (including its mast) the Empire State Building is 1,454-feet-high and became the tallest building in the world on its completion in 1931.

FAR RIGHT: An Art Deco masterpiece, the building proved an immediate success with New Yorkers and tourists who flocked to see the city from the building's observatories, though due to the Great Depression many of its offices stood empty for some years. Since the destruction of the World Trade Center, it is again the tallest building in the city and an essential part of the world famous skyline.

RIGHT: The Empire State's mast was designed for dirigibles to dock and unload passengers. However, the airship disasters of the 1930s quickly removed the likelihood that it would ever see use.

The building's steel framework was assembled in just under five months and over ten million bricks were used for the façade. The speed with which it rose was mainly due to much of the building work being prefabricated, meaning that workers could fit each part into place quicly and simply.

LEFT: The General Electric Building at 570 Lexington Avenue was designed in 1931 by the architectural firm of Cross & Cross. The exquisite slender Art Deco tower was an instant favourite with New Yorkers and a wonderful addition to the city's rising skyline.

RIGHT: Not all of New York's new buildings in the thirties were record breaking skyscrapers. The Cloisters, built at Fort Tyron Park on land donated by John D. Rockefeller, is a Romanesque and Gothic architectural marvel that houses the Met's collection of Medieval art.

One of the most famous photographs ever taken in New York shows building workers casually eating their lunch while sitting on a steel girder 800 feet above ground during the construction of the Rockefeller Center.

RIGHT: The fourteen original buildings that constitute the Rockefeller Center were constructed between 1931 and 1940. Later additions in the sixties and seventies added another five.

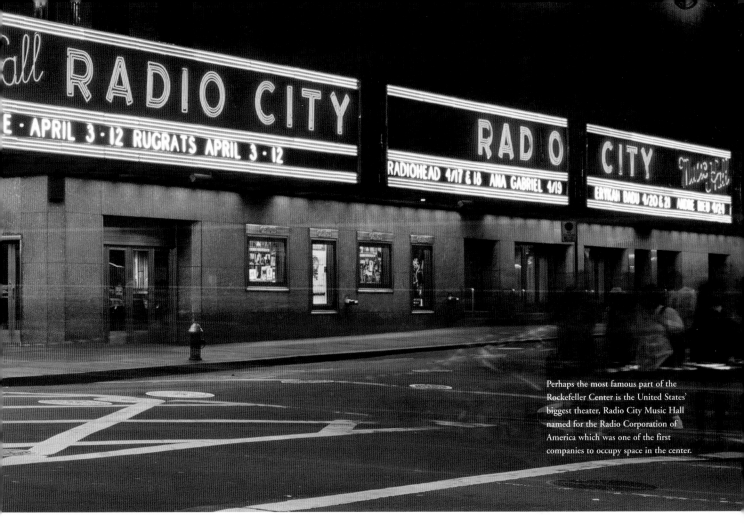

Perhaps the most famous part of the Rockefeller Center is the United States' biggest theater, Radio City Music Hall named for the Radio Corporation of America which was one of the first companies to occupy space in the center.

The Big Apple: 1940-Today

The Big Apple: 1940-Today

Over the remaining decades of the twentieth century and into the new millennium, New York has become firmly established as one of the world's most important cities, both economically and culturally. The past seventy years have not always been easy, in fact the city has been rocked by the most devastating terrorist action in history—the destruction of the World Trade Center on September 11, 2001—and has also endured near bankruptcy in the seventies, and a Stock Market crash to rival that of 1929 in the eighties. However, it has also continued to grow and reinvent itself with typical flair. Alongside the Beaux Arts and Art Deco skyscrapers, sleek and shining new buildings have appeared as well as highly experimental structures, such as Frank Lloyd Wright's Guggenheim Museum and the Rose Center for Earth and Space, showing that New York is still unafraid to take risks.

As well as erecting new buildings New York has also taken stock of its past. The destruction of Pennsylvania Station to make way for Madison Square Garden in the sixties, while an economically logical move, raised public awareness of the city's architectural heritage and saw the creation of policies to conserve and restore its great assets. Since then many buildings and whole areas of the city, such as the South Street Seaport, Cheslea Piers, Forty-second Street, Hell's Kitchen, Tribeca, Ellis Island, and Times Square have all benefited from regeneration work that has kept New York's history alive even as it looks to the future.

As New York approaches its four hundredth birthday, the city and its people have every reason to be proud. Few cities anywhere in the world have equalled the speed of its growth or can claim its influence on global culture. It is a center of commerce and much more. The city has nurtured great artists like Andy Warhol, filmmakers such as Woody Allen, musicians like Bob Dylan. It is not only a melting pot of peoples, but of ideas; an inspirational city whose sidewalks, cafes, parks, and buildings are etched into the global consciousness. The home of the United Nations, it is also the world's political heart. New York is truly the capital of the world.

PREVIOUS PAGE: Long associated with times of celebration in New York City, Times Square enjoyed a long overdue facelift in the 1990s and is now a vibrant center of entertainment and nightlife.

RIGHT: Originally named Idlewild Airport, construction started on John F. Kennedy International Airport in Queens in 1942. At the time it was planned that the airport would be relatively small, the whole complex being built over a golf course. Today, JFK handles over forty million passengers a year, more than any other American airport.

At the center of this photograph is the Secretariat Building of the United Nations. Part of a complex built on land by the East River that was purchased with the help of an $8.5 million donation from John D. Rockefeller, the buildings were constructed between 1949 and 1950 and are considered to be the most politically important area of global politics, a fact that adds weight to New York's claim to be the unofficial Capital of the World.

May 1959 saw the opening of the Lincoln Center for the Performing Arts on a redeveloped West Side site that had previously been a slum area. The complex, which is home to eleven performing arts companies including the Metropolitan Opera, is the largest of its kind anywhere in the world.

LEFT AND RIGHT: **Another momentous building to open in 1959 was the Guggenheim Museum, designed by America's favorite architect, Frank Lloyd Wright. Centered around a huge spiral ramp, around which is displayed the finest collection of modern art in the world, the building is a work of genius in its own right.**

THE SOLOMON R GUGGENHEIM MUSEU

LEFT AND RIGHT: From the 1960s onward, New Yorkers saw the development of a new breed of skyscraper. Reflecting a new aesthetic of futuristic starkness and simplicity these sleek buildings would set the tone for years to come. The Pan American Building (sold in 1981 to MetLife) was designed with the help of International Style pioneers Walter Gropius and Pietro Belluschi. Completed in March 1963, the building now provides a startling contrast to the Grand Central Terminal, which sits at its feet.

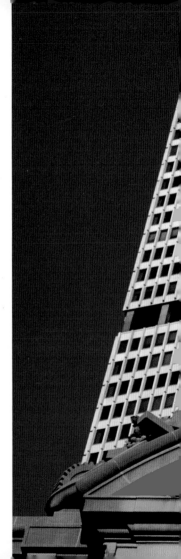

World Trade Center

From completion in 1973 to destruction in 2001, the twin towers of the World Trade Center were a focal point of the New York City skyline. The first to be built, One WTC, at 1,368 feet high, was the tallest building on Earth until Chicago's Sears Tower took the title. Two WTC was the smaller of the two by six feet. Providing well over a million square feet of office space the buildings were so large that they were assigned their own zip code. Both towers, as well as the smaller buildings of the World Trade Center complex were totally destroyed in a terrorist attack on September 11, 2001. This outrage left 2,794 people dead and tore a hole in New York's beloved skyline. While such a wound will be felt for decades and centuries to come, with typical defiance the city is currently constructing a replacement for the towers, the 1,776 foot Freedom Tower, the height of which reflects the year that the Declaration of Independence was signed.

RIGHT: When completed the towers dominated the skyline and were a testament to the elegance of unadorned simplicity.

FAR RIGHT: The two towers under construction in 1971. The innovative inner wire cage that supported the buildings' outer walls can be seen clearly. While representing a revolution in construction, the cage ultimately spelled the towers' doom, melting in the explosion following the impact of the aircraft.

Following the buildings' destruction two beams of light were set up at Ground Zero, as a memorial and a reminder of the city's loss.

This digitally manipulated photograph shows how Lower Manhattan's skyline will appear on completion of the new Freedom Tower in 2009.

Copyright 1898, by
Geo. P. Hall & Son.
General Photographers.
Nº 157 Fulton St. New York.

LEFT: The Brooklyn Bridge was placed on the National Register of Historic Places on June 17, 1977 and on March 24, 1983 the bridge was designated a National Historic Engineering Landmark.

ABOVE: The New York City Police Department (NYPD)—the largest police department in the United States—is responsible for law enforcement and investigation within the Five Boroughs. There are around 35–40,000 NYPD members (referred to by the nickname "New York's Finest"), whose headquarters is "One Police Plaza," located on Park Row across the street from City Hall.

Known collectively as the XYZ Buildings and built from the late sixties to the early seventies these three skyscrapers are additions to the Rockefeller Center.

With its distinctive angled roof, 1977's
Citigroup Center is a striking addition to
the Midtown skyline and an engineering
marvel. Permission to build was granted
on the condition that it would not
interfere with a church on the same corner.
To solve this problem the Citicorp Center
was set on four 114 foot stilts.

LEFT: Next door to Tiffany's is the monolith of Trump Tower, the epitome of the modern skyscraper. Opened in 1985 the interior of the opulent apartment and office building is a startling reminder of the new wealth enjoyed by New Yorkers (not least developer Donald Trump) during the 1980s. Luxury stores are nestled within an atrium of marble and mirrors within which tumbles a waterfall.

RIGHT: February 19, 2000 saw the opening of the ultra modern and breathtaking Rose Center for Earth and Space on the Upper West Side. Replacing the much loved Hayden Planetarium, the building features a planetarium and Space Theater within the eighty-seven foot diameter sphere.

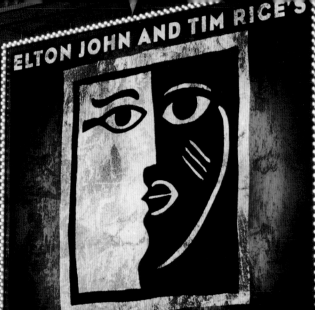

ELTON JOHN AND TIM RICE'S

AIDA

Swing!

6 TONY AWARD NOMINATIONS including BEST MUSICAL

"TWO HOURS OF JOY!"

ST. JAMES THEATRE. 246 W. 44TH ST.

PALACE

THE INTERNATIONAL SENSATION

STOMP

ORPHEUM THEATRE 2ND AVE. AT 8TH STREET

LIVE BROADWAY prefers VISA

WINNER! 2000 TONY AWARDS BEST MUSIC ON BROADWAY

ELTON JOHN & TIM RICE'S AIDA

"A BROADWAY SPECTACLE!"

TIMES SQUARE VISITORS CENTER

SPECTACOLOR

uest SUITES

Athlete's Foot

The

LEFT AND BELOW: The nineties and the turn of the millennium saw some of New York's declining areas, such as Broadway's Theater District and Chelsea Piers seen here, reinvigorated as family entertainment centers.

The skyline of the world's greatest city as it appears today. A sophisticated metropolis that showcases some of the world's best-loved architecture, an amazing history, and unexpected delights, New York has truly grown beyond the imaginations of its first settlers.

Picture Credits

Photographs supplied by the Prints and Photographs division of the Library of Congress unless otherwise specified. Map page 11 by Mark Franklin.

CORBIS IMAGES
Thanks to Toby and Katie at Corbis who supplied most of the color images—specifically.

Page 3-4 Brooklyn Museum; 4-5 Brooklyn Museum; 16-17; 20-21 David Jay Zimmerman; 24-25; 26 The Art Archive; 39 Gail Mooney; 42 Francis G. Mayer; 43; 46 Robert Harding World Imagery; 49; 50; 51; 55 Alan Schein Photography; 56 Geoffrey Clements; 57 (R) Gail Mooney; 59 William Manning; 60 Rudy Sulgan; 62-63 Richard Berenholtz; 64-65 Gail Mooney; 66 Rudy Sulgan; 67 David Ball; 68-69 Bob Krist; 71 James Marshall; 73 Louie Psihoyos; 74 (I) Bob Krist; 75 Reuters; 77 (R) Rudy Sulgan; 79; 80 Najlah Feanny; 82 Andrew Holbrooke; 83 Angelo Hornak; 85; 86-87 Kevin Fleming; 86 (L); 88-89

Bill Ross; 90-91 Ramin Talaie; 92-93 Richard Berenholtz; 95 Bill Ross; 100 Hulton-Deutsch Collection; 101 James Leynse; 102 Gail Mooney; 103 Bettmann; 104 James Leynse; 105 Jerzy Dabrowski/dpa; 107 Bo Zaunders; 108 (R) James Leynse; 109 Alan Schein Photography; 110 Rudy Sulgan; 111 (L) Photo Collection Alexander Alland, Sr.; 114 Duomo; 115 Duomo; 118 (L) Gail Mooney; 118 (R) Joseph Sohm; 119 Louie Psihoyos; 120-121 Bob Krist; 123 Alan Schein Photography; 125 Alan Schein Photography; 126 Michel Setboun; 129 Les Stone/Sygma; 130-131 Murat Taner/zefa; 132-133 Bob Krist; 135 David Jay Zimmerman; 136-137 Alan Schein Photography; 140 Bob Krist; 141 Gail Mooney; 142 Charles E. Rotkin; 143 Rudy Sulgan; 144 Jeff Albertson; 145 Charles E. Rotkin; 146-147 Mark E. Gibson; 148-149 Ho/Skidmore, Owings & Merrill/epa; 152 Vince Streano; 153 Alan Schein Photography; 155 Alan Schein Photography; 156 Bob Krist; 157 Gail Mooney; 158-159 Richard Berenholtz.

Bettmann: 9, 13, 28, 29, 33, 44, 58, 84, 106, 111 (R), 116 (I), 122, 124 (L), 128-129; Museum of the City of New York: 10, 22-23, 30, 38, 47, 48, 52-53, 54, 57 (L), 61, 65. Lee Snider/Photo Images: 31, 36, 37, 70, 80-81, 127, 154. Joseph Sohm; ChromoSohm Inc.: 6-7, 40-41, 116, 116-117, 138-139.

GETTY IMAGES
112 Hulton Archive/Getty Images; 113 Getty Images.